Usborne

First Colouring Book

Airport

This book belongs to

- - - - - - - - - - - - - - - -

Colour the pictures and then add stickers.

Arriving at the airport

Airport bus

Car

Arrivals

Departures

Car

Taxi

Out of the hangar

Aircraft hangar

Plane

Aircraft tug

Getting ready to fly

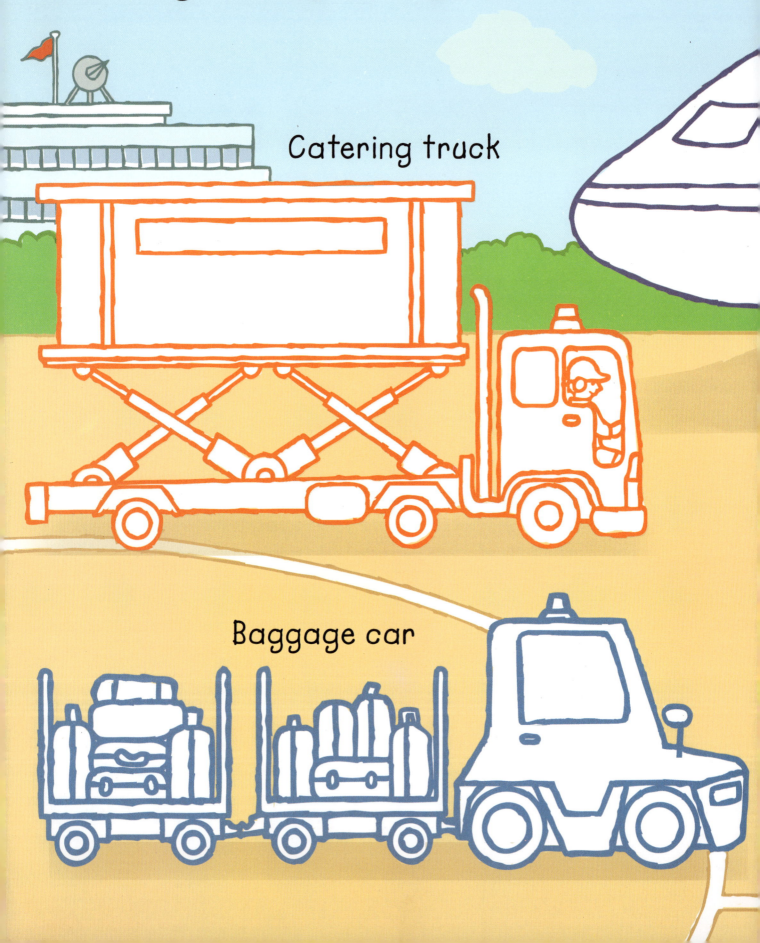

Catering truck

Baggage car

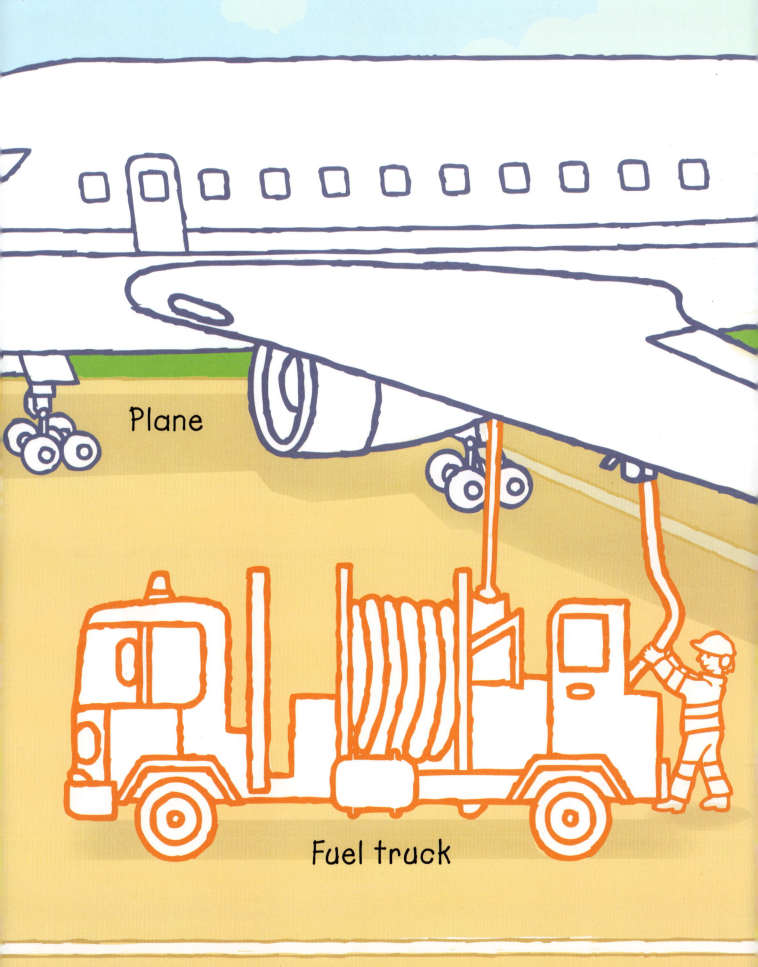

Plane

Fuel truck

Taking off

Control tower

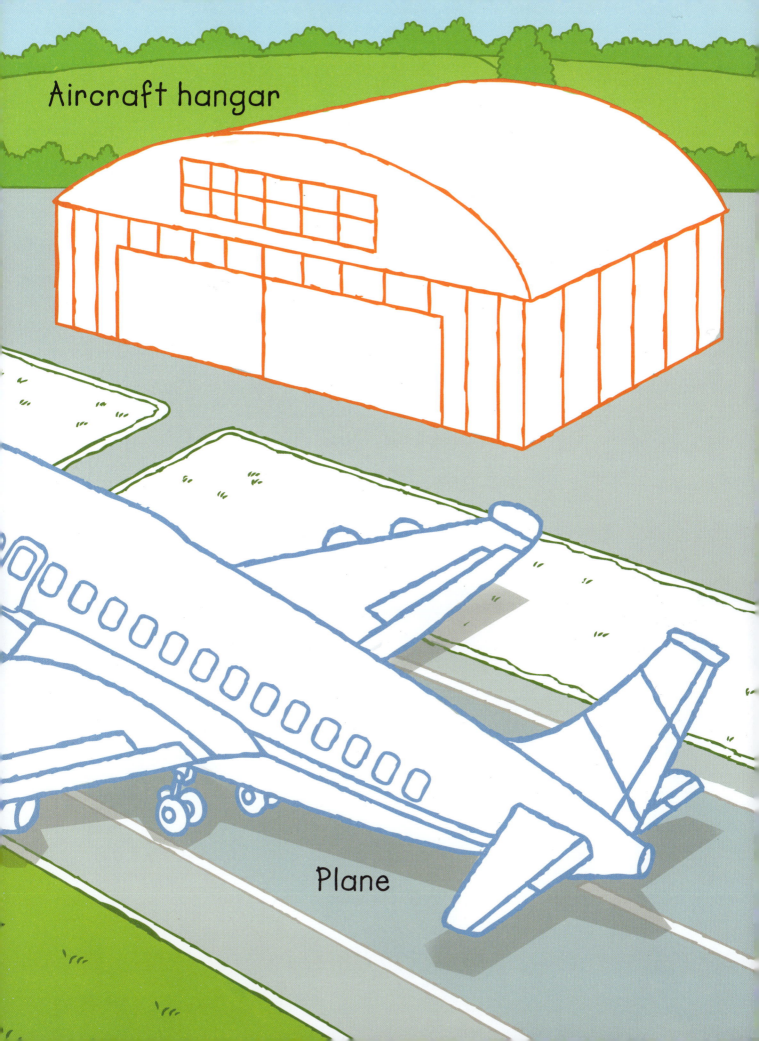

Aircraft hangar

Plane

Up in the air

Planes

All kinds of planes

Private jet

Propeller planes

Biplane

Jetliners

Lots of airport trucks

Transfer bus

Baggage conveyor

Follow me truck

Fire truck

Waste disposal truck

Customs van

Fuel truck

Can you help the plane get to the runway?